YOU'RE *cute*

i'd like to

BUY YOU A DRINK.

YOU'RE cute

YOU'RE *cute*

this is me

FLIRTING

with you

YOU'RE cute

WOULD YOU

introduce me

TO YOUR FRIEND?

YOU'RE *cute*

i'm single.
ARE YOU?

☐ YES
☐ NO

YOU'RE cute

YOU'RE cute

NEVER HAVE I EVER ...

ARE YOU A CAT ~~OR~~ DOG PERSON? ● meow ● bark

YOU'RE cute

what's your FAVORITE midnight snack?

YOU'RE cute

YOU'RE cute

IF YOU WERE STUCK ON A DESERT ISLAND,
WHAT THREE THINGS WOULD YOU BRING?

1. _____ 2. _____

3. _____

YOU'RE cute

REDEEM THIS CARD FOR:

YOU'RE *cute*

if you could have

ANY SUPER POWER

what would it be?

YOU'RE cute

the ball is now in your court.

YOU'RE cute

YOU'RE cute

WHAT'S THE WORST PICK-UP
LINE you've ever heard?